THE SEARCH FOR OTHER EARTHS™

ALIENS AT HOME

STUDYING EXTREME ENVIRONMENT SPECIES TO LEARN ABOUT EXTRATERRESTRIAL LIFE

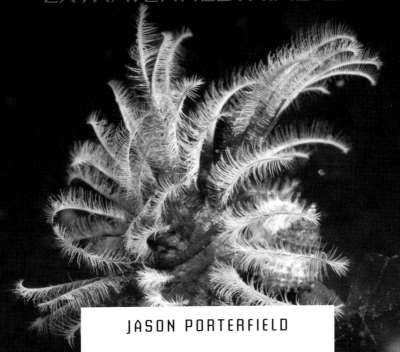

JASON PORTERFIELD

ROSEN
PUBLISHING

NEW YORK

Published in 2016 by The Rosen Publishing Group, Inc.
29 East 21st Street, New York, NY 10010

Copyright © 2016 by The Rosen Publishing Group, Inc.

First Edition

Library of Congress Cataloging-in-Publication Data

Porterfield, Jason, author.
Aliens at home : studying extreme environment species to learn about
  extraterrestrial life / Jason Porterfield. — First edition.
    pages cm. — (The search for other Earths)
Includes bibliographical references and index.
 ISBN 9781499462975 (library bound)
1. Extreme environments—Juvenile literature. 2. Extreme environments—Microbi-
ology—Juvenile literature. 3. Life on other planets—Juvenile literature. I. Title.
 LCC GB58 .P58 2016
 578.75/8--dc23

                                                                  2015033904

Manufactured in China

CONTENTS

centimeters

0   10   20   30   40   50

As far as humans know, Earth is a wholly unique planet in the universe. Our planet has all of the conditions necessary for life as we know it, including a breathable atmosphere, a plentiful supply of water, and chemical compounds considered vital for the development of organisms. Everything about the planet is situated just right, from Earth's distance from the sun to the makeup of its core. Life-forms have developed to live in many different types of habitats, from the world's oceans to fresh water and tropical jungles to grasslands. There are organisms that live in very cold places, underground, and at high altitudes.

Extremophiles are organisms that live and thrive in environments that are even more extreme—places where scientists may have once thought life could not possibly exist. Some extremophiles are complex organisms, such as insects that

This rock shows patterns on the surface of Mars. Scientists believe these patterns formed long ago when flowing water deposited sediments on a lake bed.

live in deserts or fish that survive near the bottom of the ocean. The life-forms that survive the harshest conditions, such as the high temperatures and toxic chemicals present around hydrothermal vents, are simpler organisms that usually consist of only one cell. They inhabit environments deep underground, in the driest parts of the world, inside nearly solid rock, and in ocean waters where the temperature approaches freezing. Some extremophiles can withstand a lack of oxygen, high levels of pressure, and the presence of elements that would poison many other organisms.

Some scientists study extremophiles in order to figure out not just how life formed on this planet, but also how organisms might develop on other worlds. These astrobiologists look at objects in space that might have conditions that are favorable for the development of life. Extremophiles help them understand what life might look like on other worlds, particularly simple, single-celled life-forms that could exist on planets or moons in our own solar system. Discovering traces of these organisms on moons, comets, or asteroids could confirm that the necessary elements for life are out in space and that organisms could potentially form on other worlds.

Looking at how extremophiles interact with our own world also gives scientists the markers they may need for determining what kind of signifiers to look for on worlds with compositions that are very different from Earth. The presence of oxygen and methane in a planet's atmosphere, for example, could be a sign that organisms are converting minerals to energy on or below its surface.

Scientists have made great gains in their search for extraterrestrial life. From the time that the National Aeronautical and Space Administration (NASA) sent Mariner 2—the first unmanned space probe—to Venus in 1962 to the data that the Curiosity and Opportunity Mars rovers have gathered from that planet's surface, efforts to find extreme life on other planets have improved and intensified. By looking at life-forms on Earth, scientists gain more knowledge for their search for organisms on more distant worlds.

CHAPTER ONE

NECESSITIES FOR LIFE

Human beings have a few basic requirements for life. People need food and nutrients, water, and shelter from the elements. Humans also have the ability to change their environment in order to manage many of these requirements. People pump water from deep underground and grow crops for food, for example. This ability to adapt has helped people inhabit all manner of environments, from the cold of the Arctic Circle to the hot dry lands of South America's

Atacama Desert. Other complex organisms— including fish, birds, reptiles, other mammals, invertebrates, plants, and fungi—have similar requirements to varying degrees but lack our

The Atacama Desert is an extremely dry and inhospitable environment located along the western coast of South America, between the Andes Mountains and the Pacific Ocean.

ability to alter the world around us. Mammals that thrive in one type of environment may not be able to survive in another, and they can't do much to change their surroundings. Similarly, plants that have adapted to live in a dry climate would be unable to survive in a region that receives a lot of rain.

The world is also full of microscopic creatures that have far simpler physical structures and fewer requirements. Their simpler physical makeup has allowed them to adapt to an amazing array of environments. Life on this planet evolved from these simple organisms, and it is this type of life-form—rather than more complex or intelligent life-forms—that scientists look for when they gather data from space.

INSIDE A CELL

Every living thing is made up of cells. Cells are tiny pouches that contain the biological pieces that are needed for an organism to live. These components are held together by cell walls. Complex organisms, such as animals, plants, fungi, and protists—one-celled organisms that live on their own or in colonies—consist of eukaryotic cells, while simpler life-forms such as bacteria are made up of prokaryotic cells. Deoxyribonucleic acid (DNA) is the genetic material for both types of cells. However, in prokaryotic cells the DNA is single-stranded, free-floating, and circular.

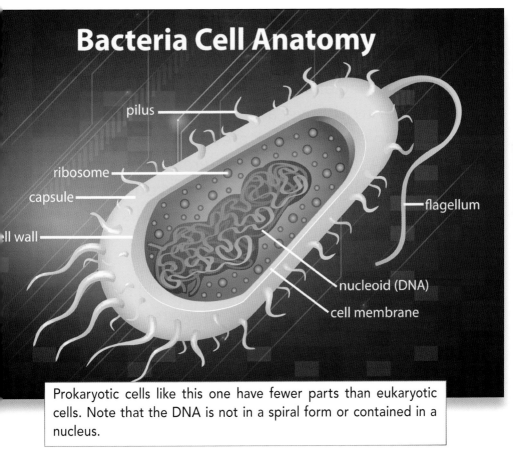

Bacteria Cell Anatomy

pilus

ribosome

capsule

ll wall

flagellum

nucleoid (DNA)

cell membrane

Prokaryotic cells like this one have fewer parts than eukaryotic cells. Note that the DNA is not in a spiral form or contained in a nucleus.

In eukaryotic cells, DNA is double-stranded, linear, and surrounded by a cell part called a nucleus, which is bound by a membrane. Eukaryotes have other parts, as well. These include macromolecules—large, complex molecules such as proteins—as well as specialized structures, such as mitochondria, called organelles.

In complex organisms, each cell has a certain purpose. In turn, the organelles in each cell also have specific jobs. There are skin cells, tissue cells, blood cells, brain cells, and so forth. Specialized cells make it easier for an organism to survive and be successful. Some very simple organisms are made up of only one cell. A larger animal requires many cells to make up a digestive system, a nervous system, and other vital parts. Prokaryotic cells do not have organelles, and they are much simpler than eukaryotic cells.

There are some similarities. All cells contain cytoplasm, which consists of water, proteins, and other molecules. Most of a cell's functions take place in the cytoplasm, which is contained by a membrane. The organelles of eukaryotes are located in the cytoplasm.

Plant cells are somewhat different from animal cells. Unlike animal cells, each plant cell is surrounded by a protective cell wall made of a

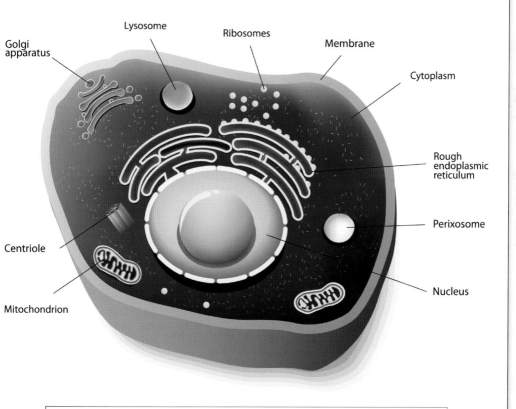

ANIMAL CELL

Eukaryotic cells contain many parts that perform specific tasks. Specialized cells that have specific functions, such as skin cells, are eukaryotic.

material called cellulose. Plant cells also have organelles that are not found in animal cells. These include vacuoles, which store water, and chloroplasts, which are vital to photosynthesis, the process by which plants convert light from the sun into energy.

CARBON

Everything that exists on Earth is made up of atoms. Each element is composed of one type of atom, and there are 118 different elements currently listed on the periodic table. Only a few of these atoms are important to life. Six elements—carbon, hydrogen, nitrogen, oxygen, phosphorous, and sulfur (CHNOPS)—make up about 97 percent of the human body. The rest is made up of various metals and minerals (also elements), such as the calcium in teeth and iron in blood.

Carbon is the most important of the six CHNOPS elements that make up most of the human body, and it is similarly important in other life-forms. In order for organisms to form, atoms have to bond together to form molecules.

Carbon bonds very easily with the other CHN-OPS elements and with such elements as calcium and phosphorous. Carbon atoms also bond very easily with each other to form complex rings and chains. No other element is capable of forming molecules as complex as carbon-based molecules. Carbon rings and chains are the foundation for DNA.

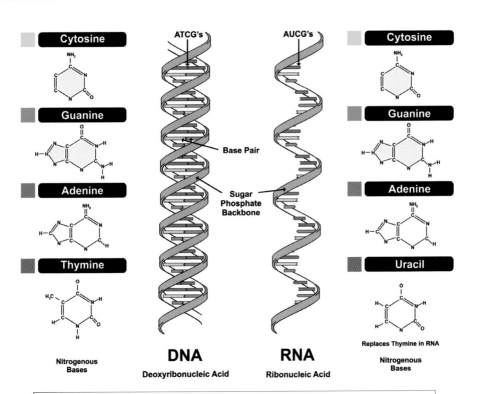

DNA contains the genetic material needed for life. Ribonucleic acid (RNA) produces the proteins plants and animals need. Both are made up of carbon rings and chains.

Carbon-based molecules are very stable, which means they don't fall apart easily. They also have the ability to react—or change—and form new molecules. This happens when animals eat. The carbon-based molecules in food stay intact and are converted into molecules that the body can use.

ENERGY

All living things need energy, and energy in some form is necessary for life. The energy requirements for complex organisms are very different. Mammals, insects, reptiles, invertebrates, and some single-celled organisms require food. Plants and some single-celled organisms need sunlight.

Energy is necessary for organisms to grow, reproduce, and respond to their surroundings. Depending on the type of life-form, an energy source may include light, other organisms, or inorganic compounds.

The most common energy source for life is photosynthesis, which is a chemical process that converts sunlight into food. Trees, flowers,

PHOTOSYNTHESIS

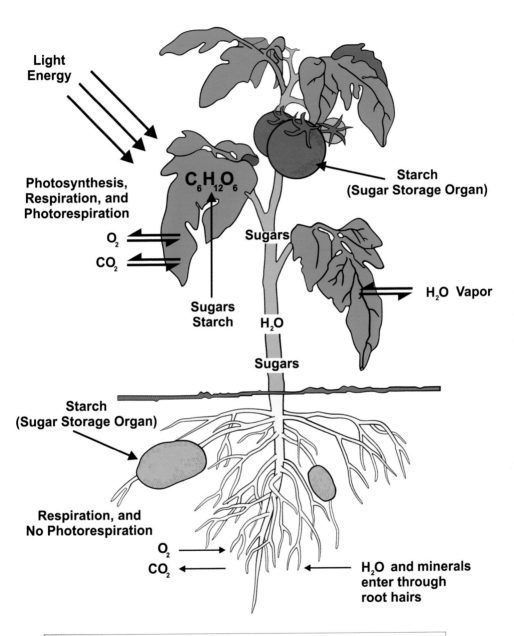

Light Energy

Photosynthesis, Respiration, and Photorespiration

$C_6H_{12}O_6$

O_2

CO_2

Sugars

Sugars Starch

Starch (Sugar Storage Organ)

H_2O Vapor

Sugars

H_2O

Starch (Sugar Storage Organ)

Respiration, and No Photorespiration

O_2

CO_2

H_2O and minerals enter through root hairs

In photosynthesis, the chemical chlorophyll absorbs green light waves from the sun, which gives plant leaves their color. Any extra sugar created through the process is stored in the roots.

17

and grasses in the backyard or in a nearby park require photosynthesis in order to survive, as do other plants. Algae in the ocean and some single-celled organisms also go through the photosynthetic process. They must receive an appropriate amount of light, which can vary depending on the plant.

Photosynthesis is possibly the most important chemical reaction that takes place on Earth. Certain plant cells contain organelles called chloroplasts. The chloroplasts act as the food producers of the cell. Chloroplasts convert light energy from the sun into chemical energy, which is later released to fuel the organism's activities. As part of the process, plants take in carbon dioxide and release oxygen, which is necessary for many other life-forms.

For the most part, organisms that do not rely on photosynthesis have to eat other organisms in order to get the energy they need to survive. The organisms that initially eat a plant are called primary consumers, and they in turn may be eaten by secondary consumers. For example, an insect that eats a plant may be eaten by a larger insect, which is then eaten by a small mammal that is itself eaten by a larger mammal and so on.

Insects, mammals, reptiles, birds, fish, and other complex organisms convert food into energy in a way that is very different from photosynthesis. Animal digestive systems break down food into its smallest molecules and nutrients, such as glucose. When the animal breathes in oxygen, these nutrients enter the bloodstream and are carried to where they are needed. Animal cells have organelles called mitochondria that convert the sugars and nutrients found in food into a useable form of energy during a process called cellular respiration. Some cells, such as muscle cells, use a lot of energy and therefore have a large number of mitochondria. Neurons—cells that transmit nerve impulses—do not need as much energy and have fewer mitochondria. A cell that is not getting enough energy can also grow more mitochondria.

WATER

Water is necessary for life on Earth. Without it in all of its various forms, life as it exists today would cease. The first living organisms formed in water many millions of years ago. Like energy, needs vary between different species, as does the way in which water is used. Cells need a liquid environment in order to survive.

Eukaryotic and prokaryotic cells need water to carry out the chemical reactions that occur in the cytoplasm, which includes water. A liquid environment brings in the nutrients cells require and carries away their waste. Simpler prokaryotic cells can live in external bodies of water, such as oceans, ponds, rivers, or even puddles, as can simple, single-celled eukaryotes such as certain types of algae. With multicellular organisms such as plants and animals, the liquid has to be internal, such as the sap inside a tree or the blood in a

mammal. The type and quality of water needed can vary. Some organisms can live only in salt water or in water that is above or below a certain temperature.

Scientists have discovered specialized life-forms in some of the hot springs located in Yellowstone National Park, despite the extremely high temperature and acidity of the water.

AMAZING TARDIGRADES

Tardigrades are a class of microscopic animals that can be found in nearly any environment. These tiny micro-animals have segmented bodies and eight legs. They are often called "water bears" because their move-ments resemble a bear walking. Hundreds of species have been found on all seven continents. As their nick-

Under a microscope, tardigrades look like clumsy bears. Despite their appearance, these remarkable organisms are among the most adaptable life-forms on earth.

name suggests, many species can be found in oceans and other bodies of water. On land, they can be found in almost any environment where moss or lichen grows.

Scientists have learned that tardigrades can survive spending time in the cold vacuum of space. In 2007, a team of European researchers sent a group of tardigrades into space to orbit Earth on the outside of a rocket for ten days. When the rocket was recovered, the researchers found that 68 percent of the tiny animals survived. Tardigrades can survive for long periods of time without water by going dormant. Their bodies dry out like a sponge. On land, tardigrades have been known to survive in this suspended state for ten years. They can then be revived from this state with only a little water. Researchers think that this adaptation helped them survive their journey into space. Similar creatures may also be able to live in space in a dormant state.

AIR, LIGHT, AND SPACE

Many organisms also need air and light. Plants require carbon dioxide in order for photosynthesis to take place. They release oxygen as a waste product. Animals, in turn, need oxygen in order for their cells to carry out basic functions. Even organisms that live under water are equipped to "breathe" in oxygen found in water molecules. A small number of micro-organisms cannot live in an oxygen-rich environment. Organisms such as these are among the life-forms scientists study to get an idea of how life might exist in alien environments.

Light from the sun is essential for plants and other organisms that rely on photosynthesis. Without the energy they convert from the sun, plant cells die. Light is also important to many animals, as well. Humans, for example, get vitamin D from exposure to sunlight.

Trees need light and air to live. They also need space to grow and spread their roots beneath the soil so that they can collect more water and sunlight.

Organisms, particularly plants, also need space in which to grow. Without adequate space, plants may not be able to access the light and nutrients they need to remain healthy. Animals, in turn, must have space in which to find the food they need and locate mates in order for the species to survive and thrive.

Scientists look at extremophiles to figure out how life must exist on other planets. Extremophiles often have very different requirements for life than other organisms. These life-forms thrive in extreme environments that may be subject to higher levels of atmospheric pressure, poisonous chemicals, salinity, dryness, or cold than most organisms can tolerate. Air, light, space, and even water may not be necessary for them, or they are required in very small amounts. They may also be able to process chemical compounds for energy, rather than relying on external food sources or photosynthesis. By looking at how these organisms live, scientists hope to find new ways of examining objects in space for signs of life.

CHAPTER TWO

FINDING LIFE ON OTHER WORLDS

Humans have been wondering whether life exists on other worlds for millennia. At first, people looked to the moon and Mars, speculating that alien creatures may live on those celestial bodies. Geologic features on Mars even resembled canals and other human structures. Later, attention turned to other planets in the solar system. It was imagined that the dense atmosphere of Venus might hide oceans and a world of unknown life. Researchers still look to Titan—a moon of Saturn—and Europa—one of Jupiter's moons— as places where life might exist.

Since the 1990s, astronomers have identified nearly 2,000 planets outside the solar system, called exoplanets. Many are both exotic and

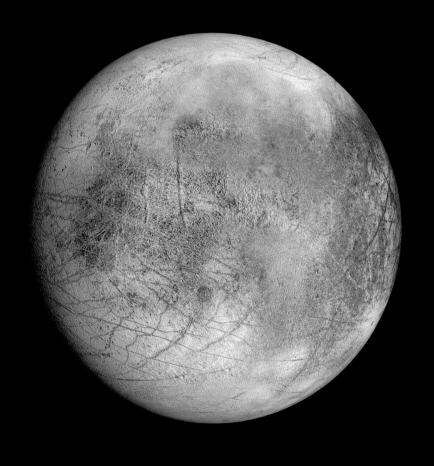

Jupiter's frozen moon Europa resembles Earth in some ways. It is rocky with an iron core, and scientists believe there could be liquid water beneath its icy crust.

similar in some ways to Earth, but a "twin Earth" capable of supporting life has not yet been found. This hypothetical world would have liquid water, an atmosphere, and the same rocky composition as Earth. Science fiction books and movies often populate alien worlds with plants and animals similar to those on Earth. It is entirely possible that some of these worlds harbor life. In 2015, scientists announced that Kepler 452b, an exoplanet located about 1,400 light-years away, has the potential to be "Earth 2.0" given its size, distance from a sun-like star it orbits, and moderate temperatures. However, it's hard to tell what a planet is like when it is located light-years away.

Life exists on Earth only because of a set of very specific conditions. Even slight differences, such as a greater distance from the sun, could have resulted in life developing in a very different way, or not at all. Understanding Earth's unique characteristics, as well as data on other objects in the solar system, can help scientists in their search for planets in other star systems that could harbor life.

CONDITIONS FOR LIFE

A planet has to orbit a star within a range that allows certain chemical reactions to occur before it can be considered habitable. This range is sometimes called the Goldilocks Zone, meaning that it is neither too hot nor too cold for life. Other factors apart from temperature also play

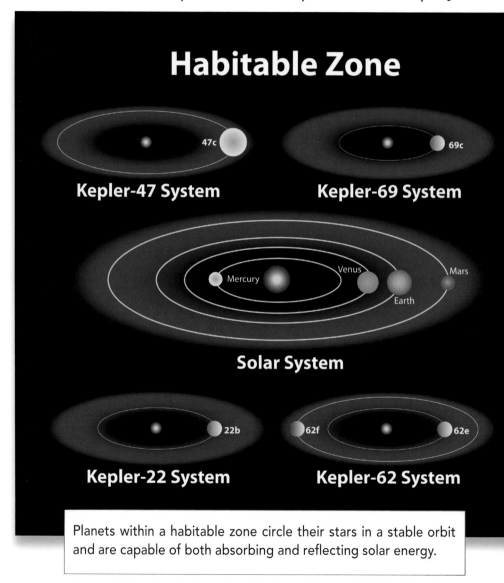

Planets within a habitable zone circle their stars in a stable orbit and are capable of both absorbing and reflecting solar energy.

a role, including the amount of solar radiation a planet receives, its rotation, and the makeup of its core.

Scientists usually consider liquid water to be necessary in order for a planet to sustain life. Water provides organisms with a stable environment in which they can live and evolve. Most of the molecules that make up living organisms are soluble in water. Astronomers believe water is fairly common across the universe. For a planet to be considered habitable, in most cases conditions have to be right for liquid water to collect on the surface. However, water located beneath a planet's surface could also sustain life. Even if water is not necessarily required for living organisms, exoplanets with liquid water are considered a desirable starting point in the search for alien life-forms.

In order to be habitable, a planet should receive just the right amount of light from the star it orbits that any water on the surface is not perpetually frozen or boiled off the surface. Each planetary system will have a habitable zone that is either closer to or farther from its star, depending on the star's size. A larger star's habitable zone will be much farther out in space than Earth's distance from the sun, while that of a smaller star may be closer.

The shape of a planet's orbit around a star could also make a difference. Astrobiologists—scientists who study the possibility of life on other worlds—believe planets with more circular orbits have a better chance at supporting life than worlds with elliptical orbits. A circular orbit keeps the temperature more constant and therefore more suitable for life-forms. Other factors that could affect a world's likelihood of supporting

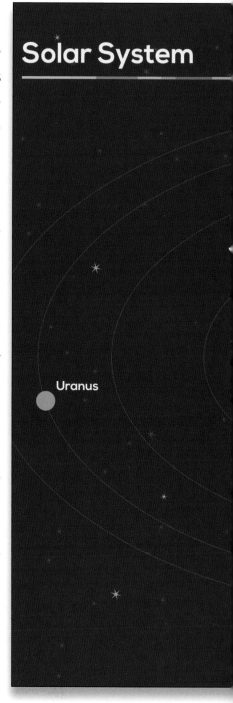

Solar System

Uranus

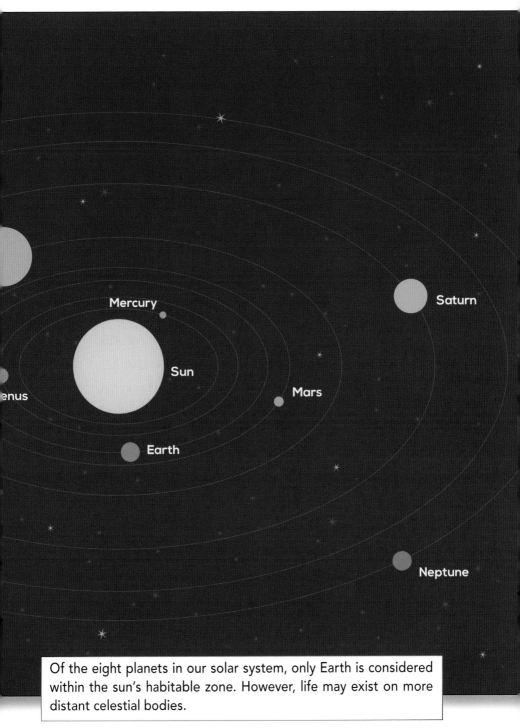

Of the eight planets in our solar system, only Earth is considered within the sun's habitable zone. However, life may exist on more distant celestial bodies.

life include size, atmospheric makeup, surface pressure, and its geologic composition.

The study of extremophiles has led scientists to reconsider how a habitable zone is defined. Recent discoveries of organisms in places once considered too inhospitable for living organisms has shown that some life-forms can survive without some of the criteria deemed necessary for survival. Some of these conditions resemble those on Earth when life first emerged. These organisms provide researchers with a chance to understand how life begins and how its most basic processes work. They also provide information about how extraterrestrial life may form on planets that are very different from Earth.

PLANETARY NEIGHBORS

Our solar system contains eight planets. The four outer planets—Jupiter, Saturn, Uranus, and Neptune—are gas giants and considered uninhabitable. The four inner planets—Mercury, Venus, Earth, and Mars—are rocky. Of the inner planets, Venus and Mars are just outside the solar system's habitable zone. Mercury is far too close to the sun for life to exist. However, the proximity of Venus and Mars to Earth's own orbit within the habitable zone make these two planets useful to study, as scientists work to figure out what conditions are too extreme for life.

Scientists once speculated that these two planets could be host to extraterrestrial life. The

Scientists believe Venus was once wet, but it is now dry and desolate. When it rains there, any water that falls evaporates before it reaches the surface.

atmosphere surrounding Venus was discovered in the late 18th century, raising the question of whether life could exist under the planet's clouds. Late 19th-century astronomers gazing at Mars discovered features that resembled canals, leading them to wonder if these structures had been built by advanced civilizations. Research missions launched in the late 20th century proved both ideas wrong. Still, studying these two close neighbors continues to provide scientists with valuable information.

Venus and Earth are similar in terms of their size, mass, composition, and gravity. Venus is also the hottest planet in the solar system, with an 860°F (460°C) average surface temperature, which is hot enough to melt lead. The planet's atmosphere is also unwelcoming to life as it exists on Earth. The atmosphere is extremely dense and consists of carbon dioxide gas and clouds of sulfuric acid. This atmosphere traps the heat from the sun, resulting in a greenhouse effect that drives the temperature up.

Very little water exists on the surface. Venus likely had liquid water on its surface early in its development, but at some point the oceans disappeared as the water molecules broke up into oxygen and hydrogen gas. More research into Venus' history can help scientists determine whether exoplanets are inside a habitable zone or just outside it.

Mars is in many ways a direct contrast to Venus. It is only half the size of Earth and has a very thin atmosphere, with an average temperature of -67°F (-55°C). It is a cold desert world, but it is also seen as the best chance within the solar system for locating traces of life. The canals spotted by 19th-century astronomers turned out to be optical illusions, but some of Mars' surface features show signs of having been formed by liquid water.

The thin Martian atmosphere means that the planet cannot hold surface water, though it does have polar ice caps. Several exploratory missions have found evidence that Mars was once a warmer and wetter planet, and some scientists think life could have developed under those circumstances. The Rover missions and other efforts could determine whether life ever

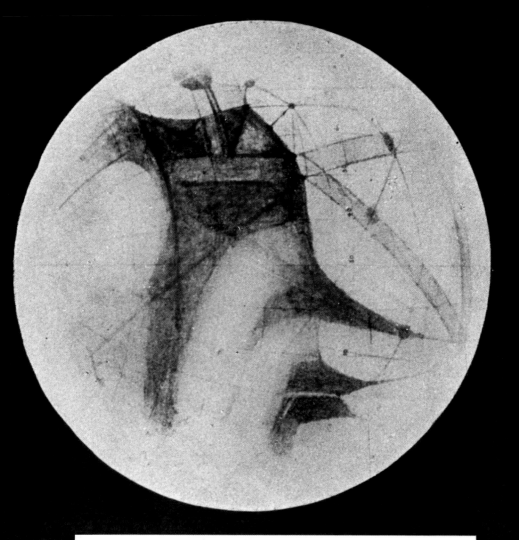

Astronomer Percival Lowell (1855-1916) made this drawing to show dark spots and canals on Mars. Lowell thought a Martian civilization may have built canals to combat climate change.

existed on Mars through fossil evidence on the planet's surface. Microbes and other simple organisms could still exist, hidden under the surface or locked in the ice caps.

OUTER MOONS

Scientists do not consider the four outer planets to be capable of harboring life. However, each one is orbited by a number of rocky moons. All of these moons have very cold surface temperatures, but some have features that lead scientists to believe life could exist on them. Several have atmospheres, for instance, and liquid water is believed to exist on some. Studying extremophiles on Earth could eventually help researchers detect signs of life on these distant moons, and even on exoplanets. If simple organisms can exist on these cold moons, more complex life-forms may have evolved in other planetary systems.

Europa, Jupiter's fourth largest moon, is one of the most studied of these outer moons. Temperatures never go above -260°F (-160° C) but the moon is believed to have a liquid ocean under a sheet of ice that covers the surface. Cracks in the ice may have been caused by ocean tides, and images from the Hubble Space Telescope have shown plumes of water vapor shooting up into space. Scientists also believe the ocean may be salty, which would give it many elements that are vital for life to develop.

Two other moons orbiting Jupiter—Callisto and Ganymede—also may have oceans below their frozen surfaces. Both moons have icy, cratered crusts that suggest less geologic activity than Europa. Any liquid water would be found at least 60 miles (100 kilometers) below the surface—much farther below the surface than Europa's ocean would be.

Saturn's moons also show the possibility of harboring liquid water. The massive moon Titan, which is nearly half the size of Mars, has several features in common with Earth despite having an average temperature of -290°F (-180°C). It has a thick atmosphere, clouds, rain, and lakes and rivers on its surface. A liquid ocean also could exist below its surface. However, the clouds and liquid on Titan are made up of ethane and methane. If life exists on Titan, it is likely very different from organisms found on Earth, but the moon's complex

An artist's interpretation shows a plume of water shooting up from Europa's surface. Scientists estimate that it would reach about 125 miles (200 km) into the air.

chemistry makes it unlike any other in the solar system and could provide insight into extraterrestrial life elsewhere.

In 2014, observations of Saturn's moon Enceladus suggested that it could have an ocean beneath its south pole, based on geysers that shoot water up from the pole to a height of about 125 miles (200 km). Analysis of the water showed that it contains salts and other compounds considered necessary for the development of life.

Data gathered by NASA's Cassini spacecraft shows that hydrothermal activity that may resemble conditions in Earth's deep sea environments is still occurring on Enceladus.

The hydrothermal activity demonstrated by the geysers also indicates that there might be hydrothermal vents at the bottom of the ocean, which could be home to exotic organisms.

EXPLORING THE SOLAR SYSTEM

There are many objects in the solar system other than the sun, the planets, and their moons. Asteroids, comets, and dwarf planets also orbit the sun. These objects occasionally interact with each other through collisions or gravitational force. Scientists study them for telltale signs of the compounds that led to life forming on Earth in their search for life's origins. Asteroids and comets were the source of Earth's water. Some researchers also think that comet and asteroid strikes on the surface of the young Earth may have brought the organic compounds needed for life to form. Researchers on the International Space Station have even discovered that microbes can live in space and think that they could also survive traveling on a comet.

LIFE IN A GEYSER

Some of Earth's geysers have been found to harbor life. People have long wondered about what causes the vivid colors of some of the geysers in Yellowstone National Park. In 1889, a geologist named Walter Harvey Weed suggested that the colors of the Grand Prismatic Spring could be caused by a form of algae living in the extremely hot and acidic water.

Scientists found evidence to support Weed's theory in 1969, when they identified heat-resistant bacteria called *Thermus aquaticus*. The bacteria belong to a group of usually single-celled organisms called thermophiles, which thrive in high heat conditions. Before the discovery, it was thought that thermophiles could not endure temperatures hotter than 131°F (55°C). Since then, scientists have discovered many types of bacteria that can survive at even higher temperatures. In Yellowstone, there are some that can live at 212°F (100 °C). Photosynthesis causes the color in species of cyanobacteria. Scientists had also wondered how these single-celled organisms acquired the nutrients they need. In 2007, researchers found that a type of cyanobacteria called *Synechococcus* switches from performing photosynthesis during the day to converting nitrogen gas into nitrogenous compounds, which all organisms need in order to make proteins and nucleic acids. These are the first single-celled organisms found that can perform both photosynthesis and nitrogen fixing at high temperatures.

The solar system is also inside a sort of bubble called the heliosphere, which protects Earth and its neighboring planets from the intense radiation of space. The heliosphere is formed from the stream of particles and fields—called the solar wind—that streams from the sun. Planets with atmospheres like Earth's are further protected from this radiation, which mostly comes from the sun. Other solar systems may be subjected to much stronger radiation, adding another variable to the search for extraterrestrial life.

Some researchers have been looking closely at observational data that they believe could show signs of life on other worlds. Looking at spectra from a planet's light can potentially help scientists detect traces biosignatures, or certain signs that indicate the presence of life. In order to determine what elements would serve as biosignatures, they examine life processes on Earth that have an impact on the atmosphere. For example, bacteria originally produced the oxygen in the atmosphere as a byproduct of their life cycles. Microbes also produce gases such as nitrous oxide and methane.

Signs of these types of compounds in the atmosphere of another world would increase the odds that it harbors life-forms that have similar organic processes as organisms on Earth. Scientists study extremophiles to get a sense of their biological cycles, in order to see how they convert compounds that are often poisonous to other life-forms. Thus far, biosignatures have not been observed on other planets or objects in space. However, in 2015 scientists found complex organic molecules in the vicinity of a star called MWC 480.

Other efforts to find evidence of organic compounds continue closer to Earth. The Curiosity rover is looking for any signs of life on the surface of Mars. The rover does not have any dedicated tools for detecting life, because scientists do not know what Martian life would look like. However, the rover's collection and analysis of rocks and soil samples could provide evidence of any simple organisms that may have once lived on Mars. Examining extremophiles in cold and desert environments helps scientists determine what kind of evidence to look for.

NASA has also proposed sending probes to Europa and to other faraway moons within the solar system. The Europa probe would include instruments for determining the moon's composition and characteristics, including any materi-

NASA's Curiosity rover explores an area of Mars known as the "Mohave" site. The rover used a drill to collect samples of rock sediment to be analyzed for evidence of extraterrestrial life.

als that suggest life might exist there. A better understanding of Earth's extreme environments—particularly the deep sea and hydrothermal vents—could help scientists predict how different kinds of life-forms might form and evolve.

The harsh environment around hydrothermal vents in particular can help scientists understand how organisms form with very little oxygen and convert inorganic elements into energy. Theoretical models can also help scientists look for more extreme life on other planets. Worlds without water could lead to organisms evolving in other types of liquid, such as the methane on Titan. Scientists have even devised a model for a type of life-form that could live on Titan. This theoretical organism is made of a hydrocarbon compound called acrylonitrile and would have the ability to organize itself into structures similar to the protective membranes found around the cells of life-forms on Earth. While there is no known extremophile that is quite that strange on Earth, some of the organisms that scientists have detected are remarkable for their adaptability and their endurance.

CHAPTER THREE

THE UNKNOWN OCEAN

Life on Earth didn't always look like it does now. Scientists can't know for sure what the Earth looked like when the first life-forms emerged, but they can be fairly certain that it was in some ways very different from how it is today. Early life-forms were simple single-cell organisms, such as microbes. Scientists believe that these simple organisms created the planet's atmosphere by deriving energy from chemical compounds called sulfates and conducting photosynthesis and producing oxygen as waste. They likely evolved in water and lived in an environment characterized by extreme temperatures and the presence of chemicals that are poisonous to most life-forms. It is unknown how long it took to produce the oxygen to the point

Cyanobacteria populate the waters of Taihu Lake in China's Jiangsu Province. Similar single-celled organisms were among the first life-forms on Earth.

that it exists today, but the cyanobacteria responsible survived in an environment much like that found in some parts of the deep sea. Today, oxygen makes up 21 percent of Earth's atmosphere, and cyanobacteria exist as the chloroplasts found in plant cells. Scientists study the extreme conditions found around deep-sea vents to get a sense of how life emerged on this planet, and how it might look on other planets.

DEEP SEA CONDITIONS

The deep sea describes the lowest level of the ocean and starts at about

5,905 feet (1,800 m). It lies between the thermo-cline—a layer of the sea between the mixed layer at the top and the deep water layer—and the seabed, where little or no sunlight can penetrate. Most organisms that live at this level get their food from organic material that falls from higher lev-els, including the remains of other sea life. Going deeper, at about 13,000 feet (3,962 m) the water temperature drops to near freezing and no sun-light at all penetrates. The pressure increases to crushing levels.

The deep sea environment is one of the least understood on Earth. About 71 percent of the globe is covered by water, and the oceans contain about 96.5 percent of the world's water. About 95 percent of Earth's living space is located under water. These waters remain largely unknown to researchers, even after many centuries of explo-ration. Humans still know relatively little about the life-forms that dwell in the depths of the sea, largely because conditions there are extremely inhospitable.

For a long time, scientists believed that the lack of food and light, cold temperatures,

Zones of the Ocean

The ocean is typically divided into five layers based on depth. Humans are most familiar with the top two layers: the epipelagic zone and the mesopelagic zone.

and enormous pressure levels meant that there was very little life at these depths and on the ocean floor at its deepest points. This is not the case, as thousands of distinct marine organisms have adapted to this challenging environment. They include fish, crustaceans such as shrimp, worms, corals, and jellyfishes. Many have developed features that look positively alien, such as enlarged eyes, transparent bodies, and bioluminescent lures meant to attract prey.

Bioluminescent creatures, such as this jellyfish, populate the deeper parts of the ocean, where intense pressure and a lack of light have caused life to develop in unique ways.

Conditions on the ocean floor are fairly steady in most places. Because there is no light, no photosynthesis can take place there. In areas where the depth is less than 13,123 feet (4,000 m), the floor is made up of the calcareous shells of zooplankton—tiny invertebrates that float freely throughout the world's waters. At deeper levels, most of these shells dissolve, and the bottom consists of sediment, including brown clays and plankton shells made of silica. The waters at these deep levels contain very little oxygen. Temperatures are very cold but constant, as are salt levels. Strong currents do not exist at such depths.

Single-celled microbes thrive in the deep ocean, sometimes in unexpected places. Their simpler structure makes it easier for them to adapt to varying conditions than more complex organisms. This is particularly true on the ocean floor, and their ability to live in such harsh conditions makes them useful in studying what life on other planets might look like.

Piezophiles are one type of single-celled organism that live on the ocean floor. They thrive in high-pressure environments. They include archaea, which are an entire kingdom of single-celled organisms. Archaea are prokaryotes, meaning they don't have a cell nucleus or any other membrane-bound organelles within the cell wall. These simple organisms are capable of using a remarkable variety of sources to generate energy. Archaea can process organic materials such as sugars. They can also use inorganic substances, including ammonia, hydrogen gas, and metals, to produce the energy they need. Because of their adaptability, archaea are found virtually everywhere, including hydrothermal vents.

HYDROTHERMAL VENTS

In recent years, much of the research on deep sea extremophiles has focused on organisms living in or near hydrothermal vents, which are openings in the sea floor through which heated mineral-rich water escapes. These hot springs are usually found near underwater volcanoes and places where sections of the Earth's crust, called tectonic plates, come together. They form when seawater flows into cracks and below the Earth's crust, where it is heated. The hot water can reach temperatures of more than 700°F (340°C) but does not boil due to the high pressure at the ocean's bottom. Instead, it escapes to form hydrothermal vents. As the water returns to the sea, it carries with it minerals, metals, and chemicals picked up from beneath the crust.

Deep sea vents are often classified by their appearance. In many cases, the minerals that the heated water carries with it form cylindrical structures that look like chimneys. The plume of water that comes out of these chimneys is often black due to the sulfur-rich minerals that come with them, leading scientists to nickname them "black smokers." There are also "white smokers," which carry lighter colored minerals, such as calcium, and usually have lower temperatures. The stream of water also flows more slowly from white smokers.

Several things happen to the water that feeds hydrothermal vents. Once it seeps in beneath the Earth's crust, energy stored by the

Hot volcanic bubbles pour out from a deep sea vent in the Pacific Ocean. Geothermal activity is constantly taking place in some parts of the world's oceans.

molten rock below warms it to between 572° and 752°F (300° and 400°C). As the water heats up, it reacts to the elements in the Earth's crust and changes. All of the oxygen is removed from the water, and it becomes acidic. It also picks up heavy metals, including zinc, copper, and iron, as well as other minerals, such as hydrogen sulfide or calcium. Hot liquids rise above cold liquids, so the transformed fluid pushes upward and out of the crust. The metals and hydrogen sulfide are carried along as it escapes.

When the hot hydrothermal fluids leave the chimney, they mix with

This diagram shows how cold seawater flows through fissures and then underground, where it is heated before escaping through a hydrothermal vent.

the cold sea water. The metals and minerals combine in a reaction that gives the vents their smoking appearance. In the case of black smokers, the metals and hydrogen sulfide form metal sulfides. In white smokers, the metal sulfides form in the chimney before the hydrothermal fluids reach the seawater. The minerals that are left, such as silica, also react to the cold ocean water to form a white mineral called anhydrite. The mineral concentrations of both black and white plumes are highly toxic to most life-forms, but some organisms have adapted. Some vents also have cooler, weaker flows and no plume. These are called seeps.

LIVING BY A HYDROTHERMAL VENT

Deep sea vents represent a hazardous environment even by the standards of the deep ocean. The high temperatures, lack of oxygen, and high concentrations of heavy metals and minerals that are often poisonous to organisms are believed to resemble conditions on some exoplanets. Researchers study how the organisms that dwell in this environment adapt and survive in such harsh conditions to get an idea of what life might look like on worlds unlike our own.

Scientists did not even know that hydrothermal vents existed until 1977. Researchers were using a deep sea probe to study an oceanic spreading ridge—a point where two tectonic plates join—when they came across a hydrothermal vent near the Galapagos Islands. They were surprised to

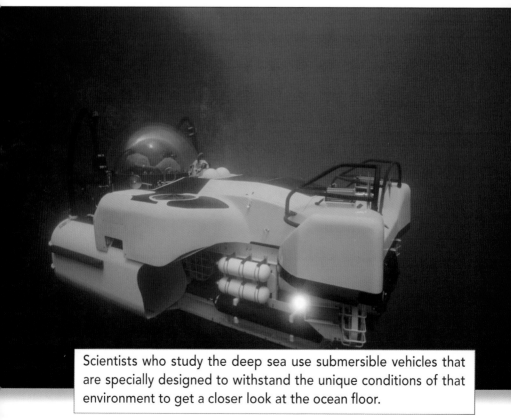

Scientists who study the deep sea use submersible vehicles that are specially designed to withstand the unique conditions of that environment to get a closer look at the ocean floor.

discover a wide variety of deep sea ocean life-forms that had never been seen before living near the vent. Compared with the rest of the ocean floor, the area looked like a rain forest. Researchers found communities of shrimp, crabs, tubeworms, fish, clams, slugs, and anemones. Before this discovery, it was believed that all life depended on the sun.

CREATURES OF THE VENTS

Many organisms that live in the deep sea do depend in some small part on the sun. They feed on the remains of plankton, which live through photosynthesis. This "marine snow" of organic material is constantly falling through the levels of the ocean, and many deep sea organisms do rely on it in some way. However, life for some organisms that live in and around hydrothermal vents is different. These deep sea organisms must depend on the hydrothermal fluids and the mineral deposits they leave behind for nutrition.

Areas around hydrothermal vents are 10,000 to 100,000 times more densely populated than other parts of the deep sea landscape. Thus far, scientists have discovered more than three hundred previously unknown species at vent sites.

As with other parts of the Earth, microorganisms serve as the starting point for life around hydrothermal vents. The microbes that live in these areas generate energy through a process called chemosynthesis, which uses oxygen in the seawater to convert the hydrogen sulfide, methane, and other chemicals into organic material and nutrients. Chemosynthetic microbes exist on their own in the water, or on the bodies of more complex organisms that live near vents. Tubeworms and shrimp both host chemosynthetic microbes on or in their bodies in a symbiotic relationship. In exchange for serving as host, these organisms benefit from the nutrients that the microbes produce.

These chemosynthetic organisms are valuable to science because they may help answer the question of how life developed on Earth. They also may give a hint as to what life looks like on other planets. Researchers

This deep sea worm (*Nereis sandersi*) was discovered near a hydrothermal vent in the Atlantic Ocean. It feeds on bacteria that live off of nutrients from the vent.

have discovered previously unknown molecules, enzymes called "extremozymes," and metabolic processes in these extremophiles that enable them to live in a place where conditions are increasingly hostile.

LOCATING DEEP SEA EXTREMOPHILES

Scientists have located deep sea vents in several areas of the world's oceans since the first discovery in the Pacific. Ocean extremophiles have been found as deep as 6.8 miles (11 km) below the ocean's surface in the forbidding landscape of the Mariana Trench, which is an underwater canyon located in the western Pacific that is the deepest point in the ocean. Single-celled organisms

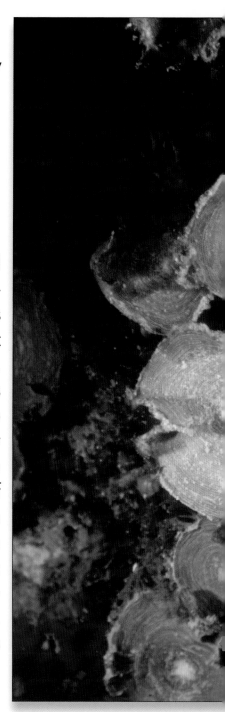

Xenophyophores, such as these *Marginopora vertebralis* found on a reef in the South Pacific, are considered the largest single-celled organisms on the planet.

EXPLORING THE DEPTHS

Most recreational divers only go about 130 feet (40 m), and the record for a deep dive is 1,000 feet (304.8 m). Submersible research pods first developed more than fifty years ago and refined in the years since have made it possible to go deeper. In 1960, US Navy Lieutenant Don Walsh and the French oceanographer Jacques Piccard took a submersible pod 35,858 feet (10,930 m) below the ocean's surface to the very bottom of the Challenger Deep, which is the deepest part of Mariana Trench. The journey took about five hours. In 2012, filmmaker and ocean exploration enthusiast James Cameron repeated the feat in a one-person submersible vessel made from a blend of epoxy resin and tiny glass spheres, which he named the *Deepsea Challenger*. Cameron made the trip down in about half the time it took Walsh and Piccard, and was able to collect some data during his trip. New life-forms discovered during the trip include a see-through sea cucumber found at about 1.7 miles (2.7 km) and single-celled xenopyophores deep in the Mariana Trench that grew as large as saucers.

Studies of the xenophyophores show that they likely survive in such an unwelcoming environment by accumulating high levels of toxic substances such as lead, mercury, and uranium in their bodies to the point that they are resistant to the poisonous levels of metals found in the deep ocean.

Scientists have learned a great deal not just from studying the biological makeup of these extremophiles, but by observing them as well. One organism called *Ctenopelta porifera* migrates from one vent site to another, rather than remaining stationary. This species of sea snail is found at vent sites located along an underwater mountain range called the East Pacific Rise. Scientists studying vents in the area found that while in their larval form, these organisms can travel up to 217 miles (350 km) from one vent site to another. When an eruption at a vent site wiped out all of the organisms that lived there, a short time later scientists found the *Ctenopelta* larvae had colonized the area, although the species hadn't been detected there before. Researchers speculate that the organisms were either able to slow their metabolism down in order to survive the trek or they were carried by extremely fast ocean-bottom jet currents.

called xenophyophores—which are found throughout the ocean—have been located there at a depth of 6.6 miles (10.6 km) despite the extreme cold and pressure. The temperature hovers between 39.2°F (4°C) and 33.8°F (1°C). The pressure is more than one thousand times the standard atmospheric pressure on land.

Data has suggested that microbial life thrives deep within the trench. Several unmanned research vessels were sent into the trench in the 1960s and 1970s, capturing images of a flatfish and shrimp, along with microorganisms living in the mud at the bottom. A 2011 expedition by the Scripps Institution of Oceanography at the University of California San Diego sent untethered cameras into the trench and recorded xenophyophores more than four inches (ten centimeters) long. Scientists believe that these xenophyophores are the largest single-celled organisms in existence.

A COLDER HABITAT

In many places, the deep ocean hovers around 35.6°F (2°C). However, there are places where the water temperatures can reach as low as 10.4°F (-12°C). It doesn't freeze because of the high salt content of the water, but such temperatures are still deadly to most ocean life.

A class of extremophiles called psychrophiles have adapted in different ways to survive these temperatures. Psychrophiles can be found in many parts of the globe, including Antarctic sea ice, glaciers, and snowfields, as well as high-altitude bodies of water. Most psychrophiles are archaea or bacteria. They can survive such low temperatures because their cell membranes are resistant to stiffening in the cold. Some forms of psychrophiles have

Deep sea fish, such as the blackfin icefish, are among the larger organisms that can survive in extreme conditions. This unique species lacks red blood cells.

glycerol or antifreeze proteins that can lower the freezing point of water by several degrees, allowing them to survive in circumstances that would have frozen other cells.

Some larger organisms are also classified as psychrophiles. Certain frogs and turtles, for example, have special proteins in their bodies that speed up the freezing process. When their body liquids start freezing, the proteins are activated and the animal's body freezes very quickly. By doing so, their bodies prevent a slow freeze that could result in ice crystals forming inside and damaging organs and other structures. The organisms survive in a dormant state until they thaw out.

CHAPTER FOUR

UNFRIENDLY LANDS

Scientists who research extremophiles spend a lot of time studying organisms that live in the deep sea. The harsh conditions there—including cold temperatures, little or no oxygen, high pressure, and the presence of elements at toxic levels—resemble what many think the surface of exoplanets or even nearby moons such as Titan might look like. They want to understand how life here can adapt to such conditions, and what it may look like on other worlds. However, other hostile environments are also worth studying, since such a variety of different kinds of exoplanets have been found so far. Extremophiles can be found in deserts, deep underground, in ice, and at high altitudes.

THE DESERT ENVIRONMENT

Humans have lived in and near deserts for thousands of years but are just beginning to understand how complex and delicate life can be in desert biomes. For centuries, deserts have been ignored as wastelands by many people, apart from the hardy groups who lived in them and the occasional researcher or explorer. In some desert environments, such

Deserts often look empty, but many plants, animals, and insects inhabit them. Looking at desert extremophiles helps scientists understand how life might exist on planets with little or no water.

as the American Southwest, large-scale efforts have been made to bring water to the land. In other places, desert lands continue to expand through drought, soil erosion, and changing climate patterns.

Depending on conditions, deserts can be home to a multitude of life-forms. Small mammals and reptiles, insects, and specially adapted plants make use of the water and resources available. Birds pass overhead, touching down at occasional streams and watering holes. Larger mammals, such as camels, follow well-worn paths to and from water sources.

Scientists look at the ways in which these animals have adapted to deal with harsh conditions to better understand how humans might live in a desert environment. They also look at the single-celled organisms that survive in the most extreme deserts, in areas where temperatures may shift from intense heat to biting cold and where rain seldom falls.

Simply put, deserts are exceptionally dry places. In a desert, rain may not fall for many months or even years. When rain does fall, there is little in the way of topsoil or plant life to help hold it in the ground. More water is lost to evaporation than can be gained through rainfall. Factors such as wind and high altitude can play a role in how quickly water is lost in a desert environment.

There are four basic types of deserts: hot and dry, cold, semi-arid, and coastal. Hot and dry deserts experience high temperatures throughout the year, with little rainfall. Daytime temperatures may be very hot, while nightfall brings much cooler temperatures. Plants that live in these places are usually woody trees or ground shrubs. Most animals only come out at night, after the temperature drops. Cold deserts—such as those found in Greenland and Antarctica—are typically rocky areas where any water exists as ice or snow. Specially adapted birds and mammals, such as seals and penguins, may live in such places, as well as some hardy plant varieties and certain microorganims. Conditions on two of the most studied bodies in outer space—the moon and Mars—closely resemble those found in cold deserts.

Snow algae, sometimes called watermelon snow, is one species that thrives in the freezing temperatures of Antarctica, which is considered a cold desert. It makes the snow appear red.

Semi-arid deserts are usually places with little rainfall, where temperatures are warm but not as extreme as hot and dry deserts. They are home to plants such as cacti and small mammals and reptiles. Semi-arid deserts in the United States can be found in areas such as Utah and Montana. Coastal deserts, such as the Atacama Desert in Chile, can be cool to moderately warm and are a suitable environment for different types of small mammals, amphibians, and succulent plants.

LIVING IN A DRY LAND

The life-forms that adapt to desert biomes vary depending on where the desert is located and the region's climate. Plants and animals that live in a coastal desert environment are very different from those that can survive in a cold desert.

Desert plants adapt in many ways. Some may put down roots that spread out over a very large area so that they can take advantage of

Desert plants such as cacti are adapted to minimize water loss. Cacti have thick, waxy skins that hold in liquid, helping them survive without rainfall.

any rainfall that comes. Others may have very deep roots that can tap into underground water sources that would otherwise be inaccessible. Plants such as cacti can store water inside themselves for extended periods. Other desert plants, such as many flowers, only appear and bloom during brief rains. Their seeds can stay dormant for years until awakened by rainfall.

Animals that live in the desert are adapted to go long periods of time without water. Many need very little water, or get what they need from their diet. Other adaptations protect them from temperature extremes and other environmental hazards. Animals that live in cold deserts, such as penguins, for example, often have a layer of protective blubber that keeps them warm.

DESERT EXTREMOPHILES

Scientists study complex desert organisms such as cacti and rodents in order to understand how these life-forms adapted to the dry conditions. They look at simpler extremophiles—tiny organisms that often consist of only one cell—to understand how life might survive on planets with similar conditions.

The two celestial bodies that humans have studied the most—the moon and the planet Mars—both have environments that resemble the cold, dry deserts of Earth. Scientists believe that Mars was once a water-rich planet like Earth and that simple organisms may have existed there. Ongoing research by the National Aeronautics and Space Administration (NASA) includes a search for organisms that resemble simple desert extremophiles.

The work of researching desert species is easier than investigating life-forms in some other extreme conditions, such as the deep sea and polar regions. Researchers measure temperature, moisture levels, and air quality in a particular desert. They catalog species that they find there and observe them, to find out how they survive.

The Himalayan jumping spider is a cold desert creature that survives in places where other organisms cannot live. This spider species lives in the Himalayas at heights of up to 21,981 feet (6,700 m), higher than any other species. Since no other animals live at such a height, the species has adapted to jump into the air and catch frozen insects that the wind blows up the mountains.

The desert ants that live in Africa's Sahara Desert are another example of an extreme environment species. They are considered one of the most heat tolerant organisms in the world. Unlike

Jumping spiders are found throughout the world, from the tropical environment of Malaysia to the cold extremes of the Himalayas. Scientists study them to understand their adaptability.

many desert organisms, the Sahara desert ant comes out into the open during the hottest part of the day, when temperatures can reach 140°F (60°C). At this time, they can collect the remains of insects that died from exposure to the heat without the threat of their predators eating them. The ants stay outside for only minutes and rely on their long legs to keep their bodies as far from the hot sand as possible.

Creatures such as the Himalayan jumping spider and the Sahara desert ant show the versatility of life and the remarkable lengths complex organisms will go to in order to survive. Scientists also study simpler extremophiles to get a sense of how life might develop on other planets with dry environments.

In California's Mojave Desert, researchers have identified a species of microorganisms that live under rocks. *Chroococcidiopsis* is a type of cynobacteria, which are believed to be some of the first life-forms on Earth to use photosynthesis to convert energy from the sun. They are often referred to as blue-green algae and were among the early life-forms that built the oxygen-rich atmosphere that led to the evolution of complex organisms. The desert *Chroococcidiopsis* live under stones that offer several levels of light availability, showing that simple organisms that carry out photosynthesis can adapt to different light levels. Biologists studying the cynobacteria hope to gain insight into how bacterial life might survive on Mars or other desert planets.

THE DRIEST PLACE ON EARTH

The Atacama Desert in South America is often considered one of the harshest environments on Earth. The desert is a 600-mile (1,000-km) long strip of land located between the Pacific Ocean and the Andes Mountains, in the northern portion of Chile, with part of the desert bordering Peru. It is considered the driest nonpolar desert in the world. The terrain includes lava floes, salt lakes, and sand. Less than an inch of rain per year falls in this harsh environment. There is evidence that some parts of the desert were without significant rainfall from 1570 to 1971.

UNDER THE GLACIER

Scientists studying water samples taken from a part of Antarctica called Blood Falls made an important discovery that could shed light on how life on Earth endured during a period when the world was covered in ice.

Explorers had long thought that the rusty color of the ice formation on the Taylor glacier was caused by algae. That changed in 2009, when a research team from Dartmouth College discovered that the source of the color was an undiscovered reservoir of water rich with iron and sulfur trapped under the glacier. The hidden reservoir also contained microbes. The water's temperature is about 14°F (-10°C), and it contains about four times as much salt as seawater but no oxygen. Seventeen different kinds of marine microbes were found in this extremely hostile environment.

The reservoir of water is believed to have been trapped about two million years ago and cut off from air, light, and fresh nutrients during that time. Scientists believe the organisms use sulfur as a catalyst for converting iron into energy, and that they receive nutrients from the remains of organic material that was trapped in the reservoir with them.

Despite the lack of rain, many types of plants have adapted to life in the Atacama. More than five hundred species of plant life can be found in the desert, including cacti, succulents, herbs such as thyme, and woody trees like the pimiento tree and the chanar. When there is sufficient rainfall—typically from September to November—the desert comes alive with flowers. Some animal species have also adapted to life in the Atacama Desert, though there are parts of it that are so inhospitable that no plant or animal can live there. Most of the animals that inhabit the desert can be found at its edges.

Scientists long thought that the desert's Yungay region was its driest part, but they recently discovered another place called Maria Elena South (MES), which they believe is close to the limit for how dry a place can be and still harbor life. Researchers from the Blue Marble Space Institute of Science in Seattle used micro-sensors that record atmospheric temperature and relative humidity to study the site. They determined that the relative humidity of the soil at the MES site matches readings recorded at Gale Crater on Mars, meaning that conditions there are just as dry as on the Red Planet.

In terms of dryness, conditions at the MES site are as close as Earth gets to conditions on Mars. The site provides scientists with a perfect test ground for working with new instruments, robots, vehicles, and other equipment for exploring Mars and searching it for signs of life. It could also be used to perform experiments that might give researchers ideas about how to carry out a search for microorganisms on Mars and other dry planets.

Researchers have found archaea and bacteria in soil

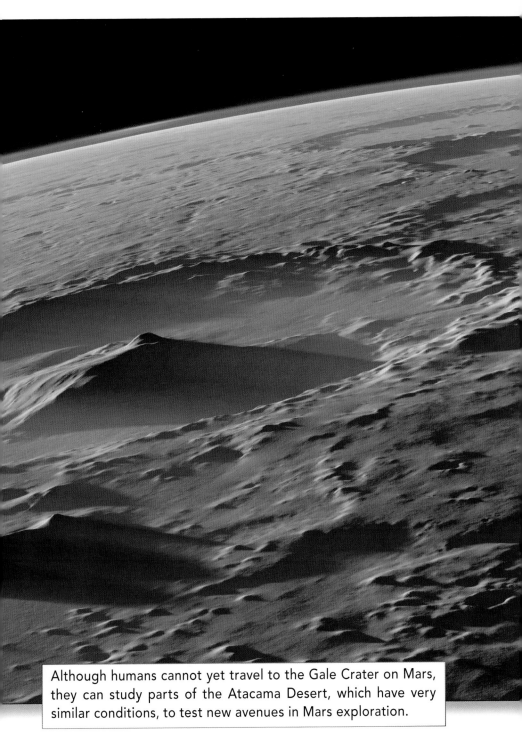

Although humans cannot yet travel to the Gale Crater on Mars, they can study parts of the Atacama Desert, which have very similar conditions, to test new avenues in Mars exploration.

samples taken 6.5 to almost 10 feet (2 to 3 m) below the desert's surface, in a layer of minerals that include high concentrations of salt and compounds that absorb water. The microorganisms survive on a tiny amount of water that the minerals attract from the air and take nourishment from the minerals, but their environment completely lacks air and sunlight.

Saline deposits have been found on Mars, and it is possible that underground hypersaline deposits such as the area where the microorganisms were found could also be present. In fact, thoughts of possible Martian life led to the discovery. A team of researchers from Spain's Center of Astrobiology and from the Catholic University of the North in Chile found these organisms by using a device called a Signs of Life Detector (SOLID). The device features a biochip that includes antibodies, which can be used to detect biological material such as DNA and sugar. The researchers built the SOLID with the goal of using it on future missions to Mars. In addition to finding the active organisms, the SOLID also picked up signs of microorganisms in samples from 16.4 feet (5 m) below the surface. Once in the lab, they were able to wake these organisms up by providing them with water.

LIFE UNDERGROUND

The soil that covers the Earth is rich in life. Species of animals, insects and other invertebrates, and fungi live out part or all of their lives below the Earth's surface. Familiar mammals, such as moles and prairie dogs, reptiles including snakes, and even some burrowing birds are at least part-time residents of the near surface. Bats, eyeless fish, and a variety of insects live in caves. While these species are all interesting, scientists who look into the possibility of life on other planets study even more unique organisms.

Microorganisms including bacteria have been found miles underground and under unexpected circumstances. Signs of bacteria have been detected as far as 12 miles (19 km) underground. Researchers studying veins of the mineral aragonite contained in a stone outcropping in Washington State noticed that the mineral appeared to have been changed by underground microbes excreting methane. Microbes at that depth would have had to endure extreme heat and pressure in order to survive. Temperatures would have exceeded 250°F (121°C).

Researchers believe these microbes survived because the high pressure stabilized their

Some organisms that live in caves, such as these cave woodlice, evolved in total darkness over millions of years and lost both their sight and their coloring.

molecules, protecting them from the heat. They also may have been trapped with a small amount of water, making it easier for them to convert the minerals they were trapped with into energy. Similar situations could exist on otherwise barren planets, giving scientists another place to look for life. On a planet like Mars, which does not have a magnetic field to protect it from solar radiation and is subject to extreme temperature changes, life would have a far better chance at surviving underground than on the surface.

GLOSSARY

ASTEROID A small rocky planetary body. Most of the asteroids in the solar system orbit between Mars and Jupiter.

ATMOSPHERE The envelope of gases surrounding a celestial body.

ATOM The smallest unit of any substance that can exist by itself or combine with other atoms to form molecules.

BACTERIA A large domain of prokaryotic organisms.

COMET An object composed of ice and dust that orbits the sun.

ELEMENT One of the basic substances that are made up of one kind of atom.

EUKARYOTE An organism composed of one or more cells with visible nuclei and organelles.

EVOLVE To change over time, especially from a simpler to a more complex form.

EXOPLANET A planet beyond our solar system.

EXTRATERRESTRIAL Originating or occurring outside the Earth's atmosphere.

EXTREMOPHILE An organism that lives under extreme environmental conditions.

GALAXY A large grouping of millions or billions of stars held together by gravity.

HABITABLE ZONE The range of distance around a star in which temperatures allow water to exist as a liquid.

HYDROTHERMAL Of or pertaining to the action of very hot water in the Earth's crust.

INFRARED Electromagnetic radiation having wavelengths longer than those of visible light.

LIGHT-YEAR A distance equal to the distance light travels in one year.

MINERAL A natural inorganic substance.

MOLECULE The smallest possible part of any substance that has all of the characteristics of that substance.

ORBIT The path taken by a celestial body revolving around another, such as a planet around a star.

ORGANELLE A specialized part of a cell that performs a biological function.

ORGANISM Any individual living thing.

PHOTOSYNTHESIS The process of converting light energy to chemical energy and storing it for later use.

PROKARYOTE A single-celled organism that does not have a membrane-bound nucleus, mitochondria, or other membrane-bound organelles.

PROTEIN Large biological molecules consisting of chains of amino acids containing many compounds needed for life.

SALINITY The level of dissolved salt measured in water or soil.

SPECTRUM The bands of color produced when light is split up into its component wavelengths.

VACUUM A space completely empty of matter or air.

FOR MORE INFORMATION

American Astronomical Society (AAS)
2000 Florida Avenue, NW, Suite 300
Washington, DC 20009-1231
(202) 328-2010
Website: http://aas.org

The major organization of professional astronomers in North America, the AAS uses publications, shares research, and facilitates interaction among members to expand human understanding of the universe.

Canadian Space Agency
John H. Chapman Space Centre
6767 Route de l'Aéroport
Saint-Hubert, QC J3Y 8Y9
Canada
(450) 926-4800
Website: http://www.asc-csa.gc.ca

The Canadian Space Agency is committed to advancing the study and understanding of space through continued research and encourages public interest in space science.

Carl Sagan Center
SETI Institute
189 Bernardo Ave, Suite 100

Mountain View, CA 94043
(650) 961-6633
Website: http://www.seti.org

The Carl Sagan Center brings together numerous researchers to study all aspects of the possibility of life in the universe, including its beginnings in the universe, the evolution of life-forms, and environments that are hospitable to life—both on Earth and elsewhere in the solar system.

National Aeronautics and Space Administration (NASA)
Public Communications Office
NASA Headquarters
300 East Street SW, Suite 5R30
Washington, DC 20546
(202) 358-0001
Website: http://www.nasa.gov

NASA is the US government agency responsible for the civilian space program as well as aeronautics and aerospace research.

National Air and Space Museum
Independence Avenue at 6th St, SW
Washington, DC 20560
(202) 633-2214
Website: https://airandspace.si.edu

The National Air and Space Museum's extensive collection of artifacts, including historic aircrafts and spaceraft, help recount the history of aviation and space travel.

Royal Astronomical Society of Canada
203-4920 Dundas Street W
Toronto ON M9A IB7
Canada
(416) 924-7973
Website: http://www.rasc.ca

Originally founded in 1868 as the Toronto Astronomical Club, the Royal Astronomical Society of Canada began as a way to encourage public interest in, and engagement with, astronomy. Today the society has approximately four thousand members.

WEBSITES

Because of the changing nature of Internet links, Rosen Publishing has developed an online list of websites related to the subject of this book. This site is updated regularly. Please use this link to access this list:

http://www.rosenlinks.com/SOE/Aliens

FOR FURTHER READING

Aguilar, David A. *Alien Worlds: Your Guide to Extraterrestrial Life*. Washington, DC: National Geographic, 2013.

Aguilar, David A. *Space Encyclopedia: A Tour of Our Solar System and Beyond*. Washington, DC: National Geographic, 2013.

Carroll, Michael. *Living Among Giants: Exploring and Settling the Outer Solar System*. New York, NY: Springer International Publishing, 2014.

Catling, David. *Astrobiology: A Very Short Introduction*. New York, NY: Oxford University Press, 2014.

Dickinson, Terence. *Hubble's Universe: Greatest Discoveries and Latest Images*. Buffalo, NY: Firefly Books, 2014.

Dinwiddie, Robert. *The Planets*. New York, NY: DK, 2014.

Dinwiddie, Robert. *Universe*. New York, NY: DK, 2012.

Encrenaz, Thérèse. *Planets: Ours and Others: From Earth to Exoplanets*. Hackensack, NJ: World Scientific Publishing Co., 2013.

Jemison, Mae. *Discovering New Planets*. New York, NY: Children's Press, 2013.

Kallen, Stuart A. *The Search for Extraterrestrial Life*. San Diego, CA: ReferencePoint, 2012.

Kasting, James. *How to Find a Habitable Planet*. Princeton, NJ: Princeton University Press, 2010.

Kaufman, Marc. *Mars Up Close: Inside the Curiosity Mission*. Washington, DC: National Geographic, 2014.

Kops, Deborah. *Exploring Exoplanets*. Minneapolis, MN: Lerner Publications, 2012.

Lincoln, Don. *Alien Universe: Extraterrestrial Life in Our Minds and in the Cosmos.* Baltimore, MD: Johns Hopkins University Press, 2013.

Meltzer, Michael. *The Cassini-Huygens Visit to Saturn: An Historic Mission to the Ringed Planet.* New York, NY: Springer Praxis Books, 2015.

Petersen, Carolyn Collins. *Astronomy 101: From the Sun and Moon to Wormholes and Warp Drive, Key Theories, Discoveries, and Facts about the Universe.* Avon, MA: F+W Media, Inc., 2013.

Taylor, Fredric W. *The Scientific Exploration of Venus.* New York, NY: Cambridge University Press, 2014.

BIBLIOGRAPHY

Astrobio. "Microbial Oasis Discovered Beneath the Atacama Desert." *Astrobiology Magazine*, February 18, 2012. Retrieved July 7, 2015 (http://www.astrobio.net/topic /origins/extreme-life/microbial-oasis -discovered-beneath-the-atacama-desert/).

Brooks, Christopher. "The Life of Extremophiles: Surviving in Hostile Habitats." *BBC*, March 26, 2013. Retrieved July 7, 2015 (http://www .bbc.co.uk/nature/21923937).

Casoli, Fabienne and Thérèse Encrenaz. *The New Worlds: Extrasolar Planets*. New York, NY: Springer Praxis, 2007.

Choi, Charles Q. "In Search for Life on Alien Planets, Checklist Needed." Space.com, June 10, 2014. Retrieved July 7, 2015 (http://www.space.com/26189-alien-life -requirements-exoplanet-search.html).

Ghose, Tia. "Origin of Life: Did a Simple Pump Drive Process?" *Live Science*, January 10,

2013. Retrieved July 7, 2015 (http://www
.livescience.com/26173-hydrothermal
-vent-life-origins.html).

Hadhazy, Adam. "Life Might Thrive a Dozen
Miles Beneath Earth's Surface." *Astrobiology
Magazine*, January 12, 2015. Retrieved July 7,
2015 (http://www.astrobio.net/topic/origins
/extreme-life/life-might-thrive-dozen-miles
-beneath-Earths-surface/).

Howell, Elizabeth. "Microbes Can Survive In
Meteorites If Shielded From UV Radiation,
Study Says." *Astrobiology Magazine*, May
28, 2015. Retrieved July 7, 2015 (http://
www.astrobio.net/topic/origins/extreme-life
/microbes-can-survive-in-meteorites-if
-shielded-from-uv-radiation-study-says/).

Howell, Elizabeth. "Studies of Extreme Earth Life
Can Aid Search for Alien Lifeforms, Scientists
Say." Space.com, March 27, 2014. Retrieved
July 7, 2015 (http://www.space.com/25133
-extreme-Earth-life-alien-lifeforms.html).

Kazan, Casey. "Deep-Sea Extremophiles Migrate Hundreds of Miles to New Volcanic Vents—Experts Ask How?" *The Daily Galaxy*, April 13, 2010. Retrieved July 7, 2015 (http://www.dailygalaxy.com/my_weblog/2010/04/deep-sea-extremeophile-migration-life-at-the-edge-of-darkness.html).

Langley, Liz. "5 Extreme Life-Forms That Live on the Edge." *National Geographic Weird & Wild*, August 2, 2013. Retrieved July 7, 2015 (http://voices.nationalgeographic.com/2013/08/02/5-extreme-life-forms-that-live-on-the-edge/).

Live Science Staff. "Giant Amoebas Discovered in Deepest Ocean Trench." *Live Science*, October 21, 2011. Retrieved July 7, 2015 (http://www.livescience.com/16678-giant-amoebas-discovered-deepest-ocean-trench.html).

Monterey Bay Aquarium. "MBARI researchers discover deepest known high-temperature hydrothermal vents in

Pacific Ocean." Monterey Bay Aquarium Research Institute, June 2, 2015. Retrieved July 7, 2015 (http://www.mbari.org/news/news_releases/2015/pescadero/pescadero-release.html).

Moskowitz, Clara. "Extreme Life on Earth: 8 Bizarre Creatures." *Live Science*, August 2, 2011. Retrieved July 7, 2015 (http://www.livescience.com/13377-extremophiles-world-weirdest-life.html).

NASA. "'Mars' Gale Crater on Earth' --The Extreme Life of Chile's Atacama Desert." *The Daily Galaxy*, May 21, 2015. Retrieved July 7, 2015 (http://www.dailygalaxy.com/my_weblog/2015/05/mars-gale-crater-on-Earth-the-extreme-life-of-chiles-atacama-desert.html).

National Science Foundation. "Life Forms: Extremophiles." Retrieved July 7, 2015 (https://www.nsf.gov/news/special_reports/sfs/index.jsp?id=life&sid=ext).

NOAA Ocean Explorer. "What is the difference between photosynthesis and chemosynthesis?" Retrieved July 7, 2015 (http://oceanexplorer.noaa.gov/facts /photochemo.html).

Pappas, Stephanie. "Deepest Hydrothermal Vents Teem With Strange Shrimp." *Live Science*, January 10, 2012. Retrieved July 7, 2015 http://www.livescience .com/17823-deepest-hydrothermal-vents .html).

Popular Mechanics Staff. "How Deep Underwater Can a Human Really Travel?" *Popular Mechanics*, August 26, 2014. Retrieved July 7, 2015 (http://www .popularmechanics.com/science/environment /a11136/how-deep-underwater-can-a-human -really-travel-17135739/).

Redd, Nola Taylor. "Hardy Bacteria Thrive Under Hot Desert Rocks." *Astrobiology Magazine*, June 1, 2015. Retrieved July 7, 2015 (http://www.astrobio.net/topic/origins

/extreme-life/hardy-bacteria-thrive-under
-hot-desert-rocks/).

Rothschild, Lynn, Ph.D. "Life in Extreme
Environments: The Universe May Be More
Habitable Than We Thought." *Ad Astra*,
January-February 2002. Retrieved July 7,
2015 (http://www.nss.org/adastra/volume14
/rothschild.html).

Sample, Ian. "The bacteria that time forgot:
Ancient ecosystem found under glacier."
The Guardian, April 16, 2009. Retrieved July
7, 2015 (http://www.theguardian.com
/science/2009/apr/16/extremophiles
-ecosystem-antarctica-taylor-glacier).

Venture Deep Ocean. "Explore the Deep Sea:
Microbes." Retrieved July 7, 2015 (http://
www.venturedeepocean.org/life/microbes
.php).

Wharton, David A. *Life at the Limits: Organisms
in Extreme Environments*. New York, NY:
Cambridge University Press, 2002.

Williams, Andrew. "Driest Place on Earth Hosts Life." *Astrobiology Magazine*, May 18, 2015. Retrieved July 7, 2015 (http://www .astrobio.net/topic/origins/extreme-life /driest-place-on-Earth-hosts-life/).

Woods Hole Oceanographic Institution. "Hydrothermal Vents." Retrieved July 7, 2015 (http://www.whoi.edu/main/topic /hydrothermal-vents).

Woods Hole Oceanographic Institution. "Vent Biology." Retrieved July 7, 2015 (http:// www.divediscover.whoi.edu/vents/biology .html).

Wright, Matthew Early. "Cyanobacteria living in hot springs flip a metabolic switch at night, study finds." *Stanford Report*, February 7, 2006. Retrieved July 7, 2015 (http://news .stanford.edu/news/2006/february8 /yellowstone-020806.html).

INDEX

ABOUT THE AUTHOR

Jason Porterfield is a writer and journalist living in Chicago. He has written more than twenty books for Rosen. His science-related titles include *Looking at How Species Compete Within Environments With Graphic Organizers* and *Doping*. A longtime explorer of caves and mountains, he has always been fascinated by the persistence of life in seemingly inhospitable places.

PHOTO CREDITS

Cover, p. 1 Greg Amptman/Shutterstock.com; pp. 4-5, 46-47 NASA/JPL-Caltech/MSSS; pp. 8-9 Jool-yan/Shutterstock.com; p. 11 BlueRing-Media/Shutterstock.com; p. 13 Designua/Shutterstock.com; pp. 15, 17 udaix/Shutterstock.com; pp. 20-21 Westend61/Getty Images; p. 22 Eye of Science/Science Source; pp. 24-25 Melissa Fague/Moment/Getty Images; p. 28 Tristan3D/Shutterstock.com; p. 30 Milagli/Shutterstock.com; pp. 32-33 Antun Hirsman/Shutterstock.com; p. 35 Ksanawo/Shutterstock.com; p. 38 Print Collector/Hulton Archive/Getty Images; p. 41 Science Source; p. 42 John R Foster/Science Source/Getty Images; pp. 50-51 Jixin YU/Shutterstock.com; pp. 53, 60 Spencer Sutton/Science Source; p. 54 David Fleetham/Visuals Unlimited/Getty Images; pp. 58-59 Bob Halstead/Lonely Planet Images/Getty Images; p. 62 Jeff Rotman/Photolibrary/Getty Images; p. 65 Philippe Crassous/Science Source; pp. 66-67 Karen Gowlett-Holmes/Oxford Scientific/Getty Images; p. 71 Doug Allan/Oxford Scientific/Getty Images; p. 74 Galyna Andrushko/Shutterstock.com; p. 77 gary yim/Shutterstock.com; p. 78 Anton Foltin/Shutterstock.com; p. 81 Chua Wee Boo/age fotostock/Getty Images; pp. 86-87 Detlev van Ravenswaay/Science Source; p. 90 Patrick Landmann/Science Source; interior pages background images (space) Yuriy Kulik/ Shutterstock.com, (light) Santiago Cornejo/Shutterstock.com; back cover Anatolii Vasilev/Shutterstock.com
Designer: Brian Garvey; Editor: Shalini Saxena; Photo Researcher: Carina Finn